MICHAEL GERRARD
AND ANDREW HESKETH

Knight Book of Science Puzzles

KNIGHT
in association with SCHOLASTIC PUBLICATIONS

ACKNOWLEDGEMENTS

Our thanks to Stephen Castell, Steven Taylor and John Hesketh for their help and suggestions.

Michael Gerrard – Head of Resources and in charge of Physics at Arthur Mellows Village College, nr. Peterborough

Andrew Hesketh – Science Teacher at Jack Hunt School, Peterborough

ISBN 0 340 19323 9

First published in 1975 by Knight,
the paperback division of Hodder and Stoughton Children's Books,
Leicester
Printed and bound in Great Britain for
Hodder and Stoughton Children's Books,
a division of Hodder and Stoughton Ltd.,
Arlen House, Salisbury Road, Leicester,
by Richard Clay (The Chaucer Press) Ltd., Bungay, Suffolk

KNIGHT BOOK OF SCIENCE PUZZLES

Can YOU answer this?
The first permanent resident on the moon was taking off in a large space transporter with all his possessions. Amongst these were a box of matches, a watch, a grandfather clock, a cracked light bulb, a watering can and his helicopter. In the spaceship there was air but no gravity, and on the moon there was gravity but no air. Which of the items would work and where?

You'll find the answer in this book of over 70 fascinating puzzles based on elementary physics in humorous situations.

CONTENTS

THE TOWING PROBLEM

Despite their economy drive, the Jones family decided to take both their cars on holiday with them, but this started an argument. Mother said that it would save fuel if one car towed the other. Father argued that the towing car would use twice as much petrol because the same amount of work was involved as in moving two cars independently. Who was right?

[7] *Answer: page 62*

WELL...?

Tim and Tony, the terrible twins, were dropping stones down a well and listening for the splashes.

'If we tied this heavy stone to this lighter one, they'll fall faster than the heavier one on its own.'

'No, surely the lighter one will slow the heavier one down.'

Who is correct?

WELL IN THAT CASE...?

Tim was still unconvinced that all objects accelerated by the same amount when dropped.

'What if I drop a stone and a feather?' he asked.

His brother knew the answer to that one. 'The feather stops accelerating because of all the air resistance on its surface, which is much larger than the surface of the stone.'

Tim thought for a minute. 'Suppose I drop my ping-pong ball, and this stone which is much heavier but about the same size and shape, will they both hit the bottom of the well together because the air resistance is the same?'

'Yes, I think that's correct,' said Tony.

What did happen when they dropped the two objects?

[9] *Answers: pages 62/3*

A BRIGHT IDEA FOR CHRISTMAS

The disadvantage of some Christmas tree lights is that if one bulb fails, they all go out making it difficult to find the faulty one. One manufacturer decided to get round this problem by connecting his lamps like this—

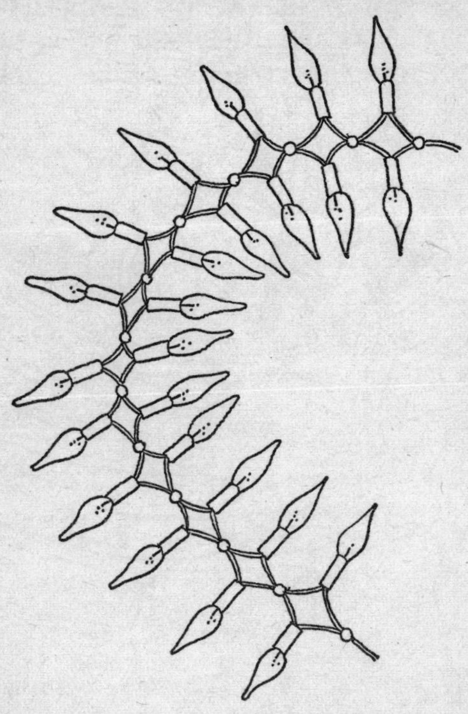

Would this arrangement overcome the difficulty?

MARY'S MIRROR

Mary was at the stage when she spent a great deal of time gazing at her own reflection in a mirror.

She realised that her image was reversed left to right. If she touched her left ear, her image appeared to touch its right ear.

Why was it, she wondered, that mirrors did not reverse up to down as well? Even if she put her head on one side her image still remained the right way up.

A WAVE OF UNCERTAINTY

Arthur Splash was sitting by the side of a boating lake watching the speed boats go by sending out large wakes. He wished ruefully that they were large enough for him to use his surfboard.

He watched a piece of wood bobbing up and down in the water. The wood seemed to stay in the same place as the wave passed, moving slightly forward and then backwards in a circular motion. He had expected it to come rushing to the side of the lake in the same way as he did, surfing on the sea.

Why do waves appear to behave in these two different ways?

 Answers: pages 63/4

IMPRACTICAL JOKE

Tim and Tony often used their binoculars to watch aircraft take off and land at a local airport. Tim liked to play practical jokes and while Tony was not looking he stuck a small piece of paper, in the shape of a flying saucer on to each of the front lenses of the binoculars.

Tim was annoyed to find that Tony did not express any surprise when he put the binoculars to his eyes.

'Here comes another DC–10,' was his only comment.

Can you explain this?

SAILING WITHOUT WIND

Mr Jones was in the sailing dinghy with the family. When the wind suddenly died he thought he would have to start rowing.

The boat had stopped completely, and there was not a sign of any wind, when Mr Jones had an idea.

'If we all blow on the sail at once,' he said, 'I am sure we can make enough wind to get this thing moving.'

Did Mr Jones's plan work, or did he have to use his oars after all?

[13] *Answers: page 64*

TIME AND TIDE

While looking up the times of the tides, Arthur Splash remembered that it was the gravitational attraction of the moon on the sea which caused the tides. This makes the water bulge out towards the moon.

Since each part of the world faces the moon only once every day. Arthur could not understand why there were two high tides each day.

IRATE PIRATE

Captain Washbuckle, commander of the deadly pirate ship, 'Lotus Blossom', was just close enough to fire on the man-of-war.

'Set the cannons for maximum range, my hearties!' he roared.

The man-of-war had more powerful cannons, however, and the 'Lotus Blossom' was well within her range.

'Fire when weady,' commanded Captain Curruthers-Mainwaring-Cholmondly

'But Capt'n,' said the gunnery officer, 'there are two angles at which we can set the cannons so that the cannon ball will reach the pirate ship. Which one shall we use?'

'Cwumbling Cwows' Nests!' exploded the captain, 'use the angle most likely to sink the pirate ship.'

What angle of firing did the pirate ship use, and what angle did the gunnery officer use?

THE INFINITE BALL GAME

Tom was anxious to go out with his new football, but it was raining. So he decided to test the ball's 'bounceability' on the kitchen floor.

He found that his football always bounced up to half the height from which it was dropped, whatever that height was. Tom's friend would not believe the results of his experiment.

'If that were true,' Arthur argued, 'it would mean that your football would never stop bouncing. It would bounce a half, a quarter, an eighth and so on, of its original height.'

Do balls, in theory, bounce for ever?

[15] *Answers: pages 65/6*

FAITH, HOPE AND CHARABANC

Alfred Grumble had unearthed a conspiracy by his local bus company to make him late for work and prevent him from getting home in time to see the news on the television.

He knew that the buses were supposed to run, one every ten minutes, between the two termini at opposite ends of the town. In fact, one terminus was near his home and the other near where he worked.

Mr Grumble found that going to either bus-stop it was ten times more likely that the first bus to arrive was going in the wrong direction.

He wrote a strongly worded letter of complaint to the manager of the local bus depot. How do you think the manager explained these facts?

AN ENGINE FAILURE?

On the planet Qwertyuiop, the Qwertyuiopians were about to develop space travel. Their greatest problem was inventing an engine that would work in a vacuum.

A brilliant scientist named Zxcvbnm designed an engine he called a tekcor which, when built, would eject exhaust gases at very high velocity.

His friend shook his head sadly. 'If this tekcor of yours, Zxcvbnm, is exerting a force backwards,' he asked, 'how can it possibly move forwards?'

WHY ALTERNATING CURRENT?

The television repair man was mending the rectifier in a set. The rectifier changes the alternating mains current into the direct current that the television requires. He could not help wondering why electricity was not transmitted in the form of direct current when most things would work from this.

[17] *Answers: pages 66/7*

MAROONED IN SPACE

Zxcvbnm was the first Qwertyuiopian to enter space. He was given this honour in recognition of his brilliant work in designing the space-craft.

Once outside the atmosphere, Zxcvbnm could not resist the temptation to don his space-suit and bottle of compressed nitrous oxide (which Qwertyuiopians breathe) to go outside.

Unfortunately, the safety line parted leaving him stranded a few oogums from safety.

Zxcvbnm found that, because he was in a vacuum, he could not walk or swim back. How could he save himself?

TOM'S FISHING PUZZLE

Young Tom was a very keen fisherman and so was very disappointed one day when he only caught two fish. However when he weighed them on his spring balance he found that they each weighed exactly one kilogramme.

Tom wondered what the spring balance would read if he attached a fish to each end by means of pulleys. He could not decide whether the two weights would cancel each other out or whether the balance would read two kilogrammes.

Tom eventually had to try it for himself – what did the spring balance read?

RECORD WEAR

A collector of long-playing gramophone records noticed that in some of his older records it was always the first one or two tracks that had worn the most.

He wondered if this was just a coincidence or whether there was any reason for it.

A SHOCKING OCCURRENCE

Little Avril Shower had been found playing with an electric socket, and was receiving a lecture from her father.

'Mains electricity,' he explained, 'is 240 volts and very dangerous. You could easily be killed.'

'But I know someone who has had a shock from the mains, and nothing much happened to him,' replied the daughter, with a hint of rebellion.

How should her father have replied?

 Answers: pages 68/9

THE MINE SHAFT

Mrs Jones was fascinated by the television pictures of the astronaut floating in space. She was thinking how strange it was that gravity should decrease with distance from the Earth when she fell asleep.

In a strange dream she was climbing down a ladder into a deep mine shaft. The farther down she climbed the heavier she became, eventually she crawled out into Australia, hardly able to move.

What would really happen to Mrs Jones' weight if she was able to climb down a shaft through the earth?

IN HOT WATER

Mrs Grumble was washing up after a very successful meeting of The Citizen's Protest Committee, of which she was president.

She had had to use both her sets of glass tumblers, an old cheap set made of thin glass and a brand new set of very expensive thick glass. On plunging them all into very hot water she was dismayed to find that her new glasses cracked, but her old ones were quite unaffected.

Her husband, Alfred, wrote a strongly worded letter of complaint to the manufacturers pointing out that the only possible explanation of this domestic disaster was a flaw in the glass.

Was he correct in this conclusion?

A CIRCULAR ARGUMENT

On her birthday, little Avril Shower received a clockwork train set and, by a rather unhappy coincidence, seven packets of crayons.

Avril constructed a circular track resting on the crayons, as if on rollers. She was interested to see what would happen when the engine was switched on.

She could not decide whether the train would remain stationary pushing the track round under it, or whether the track would remain stationary and the train would move round.

What did Avril discover?

POLAR PROBLEM

Geography was never one of Mary's favourite subjects at school, and now she found it particularly puzzling. The teacher explained that wherever you were in the Northern Hemisphere, the sun was always due south at midday, local time. Only a week before Mary learnt that if you were standing on the North Pole, every direction was south and there was no east or west. Surely these two facts meant that whenever the sun was up it was midday at the North Pole?

 Answers: pages 69/70

PIGEON PYLON

A game-keeper was out shooting pigeons one day, and was standing quite close to an electricity pylon, which had a warning printed on it: 'DANGER 30,000 VOLTS'. A pigeon was coming into range, and as the game-keeper prepared to take aim he noticed that it was about to land on the live wires.

'That's one I won't have to shoot,' he thought to himself. 'The bird will surely be electrocuted.'

Much to his surprise, the bird landed on the wire, and took off again seconds later, quite unharmed.

'They must have switched off the power,' he thought as he watched the bird fly out of range once more.

Is this the only explanation?

GLOOM ROOM

Mr Grumble bought a tin of paint marked 'PERFECT BLACK' to paint his photographic dark room. He painted the walls, the ceiling, the floor and all the equipment.

He was soon writing a strongly worded letter of complaint to the manufacturers of the paint.

Can you imagine why? What is the best colour to paint a dark room?

[23] *Answers: page 71*

DECIDING WHAT TO TAKE

The first permanent resident on the moon was taking off with all his possessions in the large space-transporter. Amongst his possessions were the following: a box of matches, a watch, a grandfather clock, a cracked light bulb, a watering can and his helicopter.

He realised that in the space-ship there would be air but no gravity, whereas on the moon's surface there would be gravity but no air.

Which of his possessions would work in the space-craft, and which would work on the moon's surface?

THE WALL-OF-DEATH RIDER

Hairy Harry was a fearless Wall-of-Death rider at a fun-fair. He would ride his motorbike round and round the inside of a circular wall for hours.

The trouble was that Hairy Harry used to get very hungry and so he thought of a brilliant idea. He decided that if the wall itself were rotated at the same speed in the opposite direction he would be stationary relative to the ground. His assistant could then lean over the side and hand him his sandwiches.

Would this solve his problem?

A FISHY FOUNTAIN

Tom wanted a fountain for his fish tank, and his science lessons at school gave him the idea of making one cheaply. He had been learning about capillary action: water will rise some way up a narrow tube.

He took two identical narrow glass tubes and placed one end of each under the surface of the water. The water rose to the same level in both tubes. He then broke off one of the tubes below its water level so that the water would spurt out up to the level in the other tube.

Did the idea work?

RED AND ANGER

Mr Grumble was so infuriated by the number of red traffic lights he encountered while driving through town, that he made a survey of them. He found that traffic lights were far more likely to be red than green as he approached.

As soon as he got home he wrote a strongly worded letter of protest to the manufacturers of the traffic lights pointing out how this inadequacy must inevitably slow down the traffic.

How do you think the manufacturers replied?

 Answers: pages 72/3

A PROBLEM IN SOLUTION

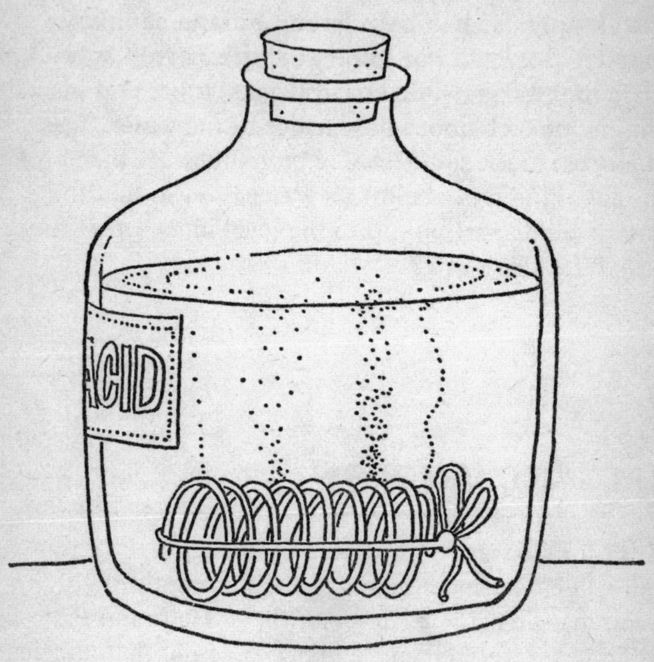

A compressed spring possesses energy which could be used to drive clockwork motors. What happens to this energy if the compressed spring is tied with acid-proof string and then dropped into strong acid?

HAIRY HARRY'S HOLIDAY

Hairy Harry was off on his holidays. He had a fair amount of luggage, and wondered if it would be better for his maximum speed and acceleration to put the luggage inside the car, where there was very little room, or on the roof-rack on top of the car.

In each case how would his maximum speed and acceleration be affected?

RADIANT COLD

One summer night, it was so hot that Mrs Jones went to the Deep Freeze, brought out a large ice cube and placed it in the middle of the room.

'What is the idea of that?' asked Mr Jones.

'Well, if hot things radiate heat, cold things must radiate cold,' answered Mrs Jones.

'I think you are wrong,' replied Mr Jones, remembering the laws of Physics he had learnt at school. 'It is only heat that is radiated, not cold.'

'Well,' said Mrs Jones, 'the thermometer has just gone down two degrees! Explain that with your laws of Physics!'

Can you explain it?

 Answers: pages 73/4

PROFESSOR SPARK'S PERPETUAL MOTION MACHINE

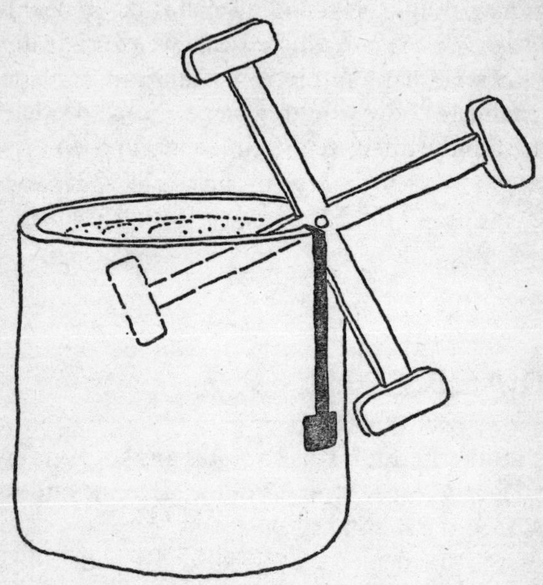

The picture shows Professor Spark's blue-print for a perpetual motion machine which he hopes to make. The wooden blocks in the air are pulled down by gravity and the block in the water floats up to the surface. The wheel therefore tends to turn clockwise. The blocks and the spokes pass through a water-tight valve into the tank.

Will the Professor's machine work?

THE WEIGH DOWN

Alfred Grumble had just bought a set of bathroom scales on the top floor of a large department store.

On the way down he was alone in the lift and could not resist trying them. Unfortunately, at that moment the supporting cable broke and the lift plummetted downwards.

During the descent Mr Grumble composed a strongly worded letter of complaint in his mind. What happened to the reading of the bathroom scales during this time?

[29] *Answers: page 75*

HAIRY HARRY'S DOGGY DILEMMA

When Hairy Harry bought his sports car, the previous owner had left a toy dog in the back window – the kind that nods its head up and down as the car goes along. He decided that the dog must go because it used up vital energy which Hairy needed in the form of speed.

Was this a good reason for getting rid of the dog?

FLOATING ICE

Tom and his sister Mary were sitting outside on a very hot sunny day, when Mother came out with two glasses of ice-cold water. Mary noticed that Tom's glass was full to the brim, with a large ice-cube floating in the middle.

'You'd better drink that quickly' she said, 'or the ice will melt and the water overflow.'

'Rubbish!' said Tom. 'Ice takes up more space than an equal weight of water, so the level will go down when the ice melts.'

They waited until the ice had melted. Who do you think was correct?

 Answers: pages 75/6

WARNING LIGHTS

The human eye is most sensitive to yellow and green colours. Can you think of any reasons why danger signals are red?

HAIRY HARRY'S ATTEMPT AT THE LAND SPEED RECORD

Hairy Harry's dream of fame started when he bought a brand new racing motorcycle. It had five gears: the lowest gear was for starting and going at slow speeds, and each successive gear made the motorbike travel faster.

Hairy Harry decided that if he modified the gear-box so that it had many more gears there would be no limit to the speed he could reach.

Is this correct?

EDDY'S CYCLE CIRCUIT

Eddy Curran was a bright young man who had just become an apprentice electrician. However, the job meant that he would have to cycle home in the dark, and so Eddy designed a lighting system for his bicycle.

He had a 6-volt dynamo and two 3-volt lamps, one very much brighter than the other. He ran a wire from the dynamo to the bright headlamp and a wire from the headlamp to the rear lamp, and then one back to the dynamo.

Is there anything wrong with Eddy's circuit?

 Answers: pages 76/7

HARD-WORKING SHELVES?

Mr Brown was busy stocking the shelves in his grocery shop. As Tom came through the door on an errand for his mother, Mr Brown was lifting heavy bags of sugar up to a high shelf.

'You are doing a lot of work today,' said Tom.

'What is that supposed to mean?' asked Mr Brown suspiciously, pausing with the next bag in his hand.

'Well,' explained Tom, 'we have just learnt about "work" at school. It is calculated by multiplying the force you are exerting on that bag by the height of the shelf.'

Mr Brown understood this, but was looking rather puzzled.

'Does this mean that if I don't move the bag at all, I do no work?'

'Yes, that's right,' replied Tom.

'Well in that case, explain why my arms are tired holding this bag of sugar while I'm talking to you.'

Tom was not quite sure.

'And if I am doing work just holding this bag still then my shelves must also be doing work. Where do they get their energy from?'

Tom was now thoroughly confused.

PROFESSOR SPARK'S PERPETUAL MOTION MACHINE, MARK II

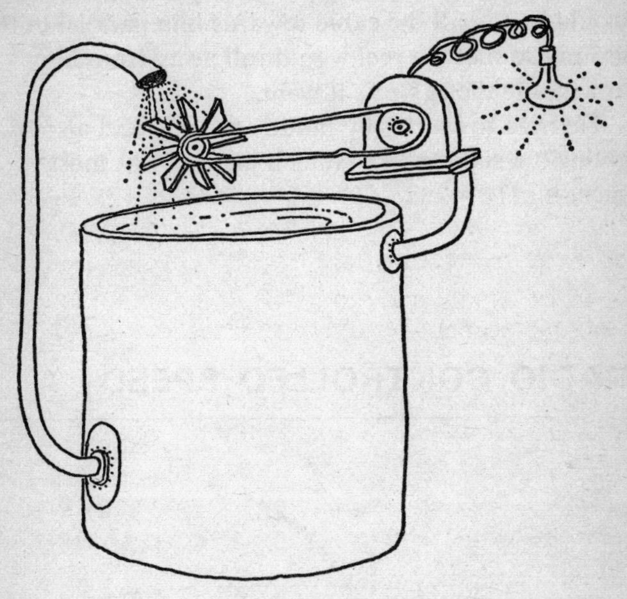

After the failure of his first perpetual motion machine, Professor Spark invented another. The weight of the water in the large container forces the water up the small tube where it falls back into the large container. As it falls the water turns a paddle wheel which drives a dynamo.

Will this machine work?

[35] *Answers: page 78*

A REEL PROBLEM

A reel of electric cable was required urgently. The owner thought that the quickest way of unwinding it would be to pull the cable towards him parallel to the ground so that the reel would roll away from him, unwinding the cable as it went.

He tried to do this by pulling steadily and also by giving it a sudden jerk. Which method was most successful?

RADIO CONTROLLED SPEED

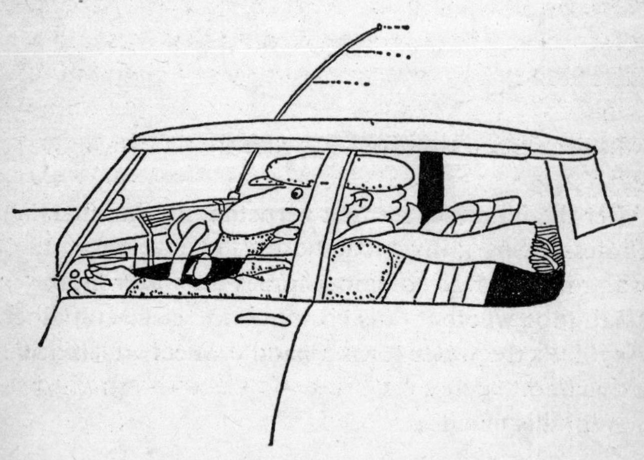

Hairy Harry refused to have a radio in his car, as he claimed it slowed him down when it was on.

'After all,' he said, 'I need all the energy the car can give me for *speed*. I can't afford to waste any on the radio.'

Is the speed of the car reduced when the radio is turned on?

GENERATING NOTHING

Eddy Curran was helping to set up an emergency generator for the local hospital.

'There are two parts to the generator, lad,' explained the foreman. 'The petrol engine drives the dynamo which produces the electrical energy being used in the hospital.'

'So the electrical energy comes from the chemical energy of the petrol.'

'That's right, lad,' said the foreman, patronisingly. 'All energy has to come from somewhere and go somewhere. All the chemical energy becomes either heat or electricity.'

'Well what happens,' asked Eddy innocently, 'to all the electrical energy if no one has anything switched on in the hospital?'

[37] *Answers: pages 79/80*

A PROBLEM OF SPEED

In a country village, the local cycling club was holding its annual event. The aim was to qualify for 'senior' status by averaging at least 30 km per hour in a journey to the next village and back, a total distance of two kilometres.

Chris Crossbar was hoping to achieve this status as he set off at full speed. By the time he reached the other village he was dismayed to find that he had only averaged 15 km per hour because he had been held up by a slow moving tractor.

'I shall have to go back at 45 km per hour,' he thought, 'I'll just about make it, if there aren't any more tractors.'

In fact he averaged 50 km per hour on the return journey. Why did he not qualify?

A PROBLEM OF MORE SPEED

Chris Crossbar was attempting to qualify for 'senior' status at his cycle club, for the second time. He had to cover a certain distance at an average speed of at least 30 km per hour. His friend, Frank Crankshaft, was making the attempt with him.

Chris and Frank set off together, but Chris was soon a long way in front. However, Chris met a large combine-harvester which slowed him down so that both bikes eventually crossed the finishing line together.

As both cyclists started and finished together they had the same average speed which was calculated to be exactly 30 km per hour and so both men qualified.

Chris could not help feeling that as he had always travelled faster than, or at the same speed as Frank, it was unfair that they should both have the same average velocity. Is Chris correct to feel cheated?

 Answers: page 80

A MINE OF INFORMATION

The accident occurred as the helicopter was winching an old war-time mine out of the sea. The winchman fell out of the helicopter, but managed to keep hold of the rope which was attached, via a pulley wheel in the helicopter, to the mine.

Surprisingly the mine happened to weigh exactly the same as the man, and so neither fell into the sea. However the initial jerk set the mine's time fuse going.

Should the man climb up or down his rope? What other action could he take?

A TYRING PROBLEM

Mr Jones suspected that one of his car tyres had gone down, and decided to pull into the next garage to check it.

Tom got out of the car just as his father was holding the gauge to the deflated tyre.

'Oh dear!' exclaimed Mr Jones, 'It is exactly half what it should be. I'll have to double the pressure.'

'Boyle's law,' said Tom.

'Pardon?' asked his father.

'Boyle's law,' repeated Tom, 'is the law that states that to double the pressure of a gas you have to halve its volume.'

'That's silly!' replied his father, 'it would mean that the tyre got smaller as it was blown up!'

Is Boyle's law incorrect?

JUGGLING THE FIGURES

[41] *Answers: pages 81/2*

Three acrobats wanted to find their total weight. As there was only room for one of them to stand on the scales they realised that two of them would have to balance on the third.

'It'll be best if Alf stands on my shoulders and I stand on Charlie's shoulders,' declared Bert.

'No, it won't,' said Charlie, 'because that would mean I was doing the work supporting you two, and Bert would be doing work supporting Alf.

'It would be much better,' continued Charlie, 'if you both stand on my shoulders. In that way I'm the only one doing work, and so the scales are more likely to show the correct weight.'

Is Charlie correct?

THE SPACE PATROL PROBLEM

The crippled alien space-craft was in orbit around the planet Xzyq. Fred Fortitude's Earth Federation Space Cruiser was in an identical orbit about 160 kilometres behind the alien ship.

How could Fred close the gap? He had six thruster rockets to choose from. One would fire towards the planet's surface, and one away. A third would fire to the left and a fourth to the right. The fifth was positioned so that it would fire towards the alien ship and the sixth away from it. Which would be the best one to use?

PROFESSOR SPARK'S BOUNCE-ABILITY EXPERIMENTS

Professor Spark noticed that if he dropped a ball from rest it never bounced higher than the height from which it was dropped, though of course some balls bounced higher than others.

The Professor therefore set about designing the perfect ball – one that would bounce higher than the height from which it was dropped.

Could he possibly succeed, and if so what would be the result?

 Answers: pages 82/3

LIKE A STONE?

Why does a stone sink more slowly in cold water than in hot?

If identical stones were dropped into identical buckets, one containing water at 15° C and the other containing water at 15° F, which stone would reach the bottom first?

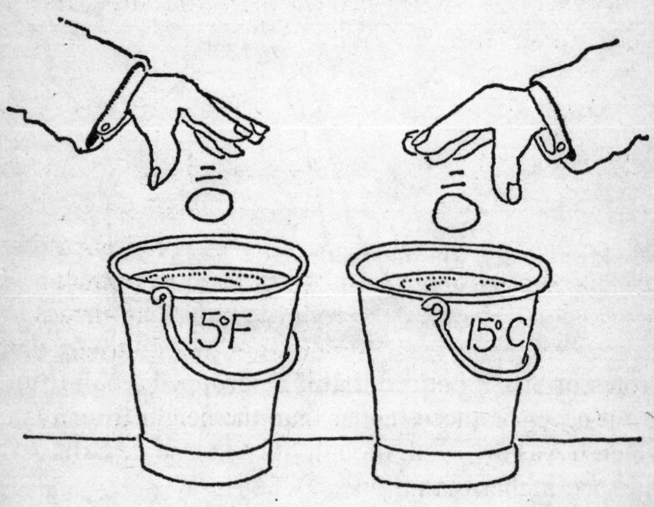

A POWERFUL ARGUMENT

Eddy Curran was helping to service an electric motor.

'The current flows through this coil,' the foreman was explaining. 'Because it is surrounded by magnets the coil is in a magnetic field and so it starts to rotate.'

'What would happen,' asked Eddy, 'if a stronger magnet was used?'

'The motor would turn faster, of course, lad,' replied the foreman.

'In that case,' asked Eddy, 'where does the extra energy come from?'

FRED FORTITUDE'S BEER

When the first moon pub was opened, Fred Fortitude, the fearless astronaut, was one of its most frequent customers. He would often sit and praise its virtues.

'For one thing there is more beer in a pint mug than on Earth.'

Then he would go on to explain why – can you?

 Answers: pages 83/4

HAVING A SWINGING TIME

It is a well-known scientific fact that the timing of the swing of a pendulum is unaffected by the mass of its bob. The only way to change the timing is to alter the length of the pendulum.

An eccentric Swiss clock-maker, Herr Spring, invented a grandfather clock whose pendulum bob consisted of a metal sphere full of water.

What would happen to the timing of the swing of the pendulum if the water started to leak out?

A MONTHLY ECLIPSE?

Professor Spark was watching an eclipse of the sun with his nephew.

'The moon goes round the Earth, and as it gets in the way of the sun's light it casts a shadow on the Earth. That's what causes the eclipse.'

The boy was quite a keen astronomer and knew that the moon went round the Earth once every 28 days.

'Does that mean, Uncle,' asked the boy, 'that there will be another eclipse of the sun next month?'

How did the Professor answer the boy?

[47] *Answers: pages 84/5*

WIRING A SKYSCRAPER

Eddy Curran, the apprentice electrician was helping to wire a large new office block. The foreman was showing Eddy three identical wires which emerged from a wall on the ground floor.

'The other ends of these wires are on the twentieth floor, you will have to walk up the stairs as the lifts are not working yet. I want you to label each wire so that it has the same label at both ends.'

Eddy was given a continuity meter. This had two leads and gave a reading when there was a good electrical contact between them.

How many times did Eddy have to go up and down the stairs?

THE DAIRY'S DAY

The manager of a successful dairy was explaining his business techniques to a young reporter.

'... and, of course, you probably know that we have no distribution costs, apart from the salaries of our milkmen.'

'What do you mean?' asked the reporter, intrigued.

'Well, our herd of cows, milking shed and bottling plant are all on top of the large hill outside town. Every morning our electric milk floats start off with flat batteries and coast down that long road into town. The motion of the floats charging their batteries as they go.'

‘Charging them enough to drive them around town?’

‘That’s right, and enough to bring them back up the hill in the evening.’

‘Now I know you are pulling my leg,’ said the young man. ‘It would take as much energy to drive the floats up the hill as could be gained from coasting down it.’

‘Ah! but don’t forget,’ replied the manager, ‘that the floats are lighter on the way back, having delivered all the milk.’

Would the scheme really work, and if so where did the energy for the delivery come from?

HIGH SPEED HIJACK

The makers of a new supersonic airliner were explaining why they expected it to be safe from hijackers.

‘The plane cruises at a speed of 2400 km.p.h. which is twice the speed of a bullet. If a would-be hijacker fired a gun towards the pilot, the bullet would only travel at 1200 km.p.h., and so the plane and its passengers would overtake it. The bullet would therefore travel backwards inside the plane, hitting whoever fired the gun.’

Is this statement true?

 Answers: pages 85/6

ROAD NARROWS

Nick Parker had recently given up his job as a plumber to become a traffic warden. He noticed, one day, that on a two-lane stretch of a one way street the traffic was flowing much slower than usual. He soon discovered the reason: road-works had blocked one of the lanes for a short distance.

Nick knew that when water flows through a narrow pipe it speeds up, and he could not work out why cars did not behave in the same way. Can you explain it?

A PROBLEM OF WEATHER?

An American scientist had a plan to change the climate of the world by spreading a thin layer of soot over the North Polar region.

How would this affect the world's climate and why did he not want to try the same idea in the South Polar region?

A TRAIN OF THOUGHT

As the train pulled out of the station, the guard started checking the tickets of the passengers in the rear compartment. As the train arrived at the next station he had worked his way along the length of the train to the front.

'I've been walking forward, so I've been travelling faster than anyone else on the train,' he chatted to a passenger.

'But we've both been on the same train,' argued the passenger, 'so we all set off and arrived together. How do you explain that?'

A SLOWER TRAIN OF THOUGHT

As the train set off from one station at ten km.p.h. a man started walking back along the train at the same speed.

Twelve minutes later the train pulled into the next station just as the man reached the rear of the train.

As the man had not moved relative to the ground, how had he managed to get from one station to the next?

 Answers: pages 87/8

THE SHOOTING LESSON

The Training Sergeant was teaching a new recruit how to use a rifle. As he took his first shot, the recoil of the gun surprised him.

'Why did it do that?' he asked, rather annoyed at missing the target.

'That's the reaction to the flight of the bullet – you know Newton's Law which says that there is an equal and opposite reaction to every action,' replied the sergeant.

'Well, what would happen to the reaction if I strapped the rifle to that tree trunk so that it could not recoil?'

GUN WITH THE WIND

A bullet strikes a weather vane, causing it to spin round. At the instant the bullet strikes, the vane is stationary. Since the bullet is in contact with the vane at this instant, the bullet must also be stationary.

Is this correct?

[53] *Answers: pages 88/9*

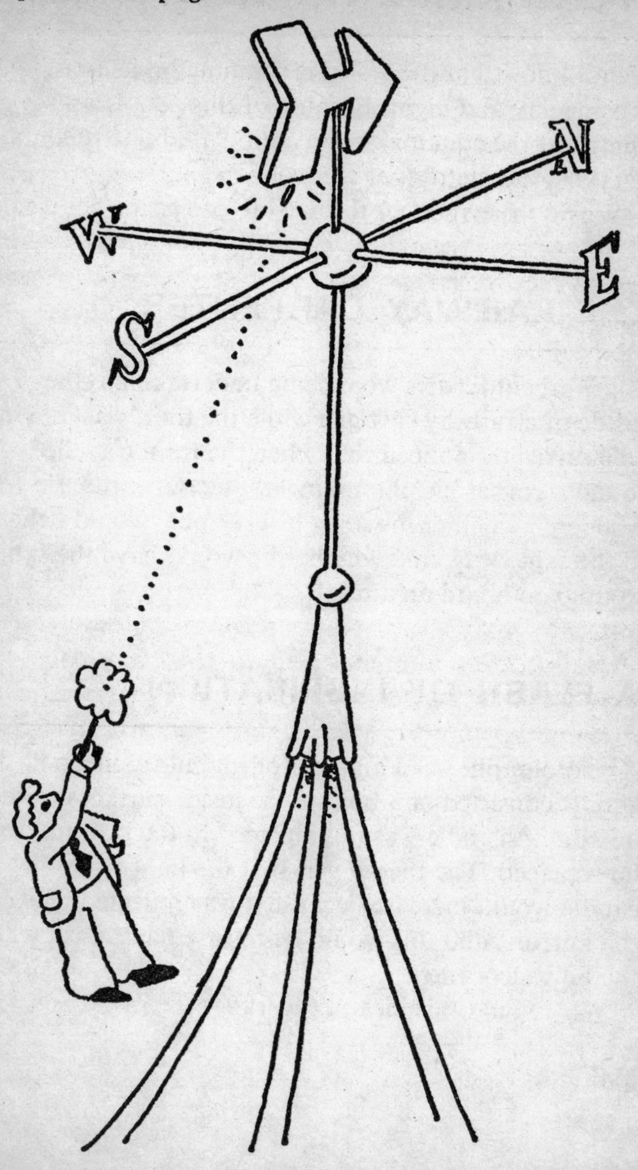

THE SPINNING WORLD

We all know that the world is spinning on its axis, causing day and night. Because of this people and objects at the equator are travelling at about 1600 km.p.h. (400 metres per second).

Why do they not get thrown off into space?

THE RAILWAY CARPENTER

Some urgent repairs were being undertaken to the inside of a railway carriage while the train was moving. The carpenter noticed that when the train travelled round a corner his plumb-line swung outwards. He wondered whether his spirit level bubble would behave in the same way, and whether he would have the same trouble on board an aircraft.

A FLASH OF INSPIRATION

A photographer had an idea for making a cheap flash-gun. It consisted of a box whose inside surfaces were mirrors. A candle was to be placed in the box and the lid replaced. The theory was that the light from the candle would increase because it was reflected between the mirrors, and this would be released as a flash when the lid was opened.

Why would this idea not work?

WAGONS ROLL

Mother and Father were watching a western film on the television. The wagon train was being chased by Indians.

'Trick photography!' remarked Mother. 'The wagon is standing still and the scenery is moving. Look, the wagon wheels aren't moving!'

Just then, the wagon wheels did move, but appeared to be turning slowly backwards.

Can you explain these effects?

WEIGHTLESSNESS

When an object floats it is, to all intents and purposes, weightless.

Imagine, then, a bucket of water placed on some bathroom scales. If the scales read ten kilogrammes, what will they read if a two kilogramme block of wood is floated in the water?

 Answers: pages 89/91

THE HUMMING BIRD

A humming bird and its wire cage have a combined weight of 2 kilogrammes-force. The humming bird weighs $\frac{1}{2}$ kilogramme-force and the cage $1\frac{1}{2}$ kilogramme-force. If the cage is hung from a spring balance, what will it read when the bird is hovering? Would the balance read the same if the cage was made of air-tight perspex?

Would the answers be the same if the measurements were made in a vacuum (assuming that the bird had its own oxygen tank to breath with!).

COOLING DOWN

Things were getting frantic in the kitchen of a large hotel, and the temperature began to rise. In an attempt to cool things down the chef decided to use a large empty fridge which was not normally used. He plugged it in and left it running with the door open.

When the manager saw it he laughed saying that it would make no difference because as much heat was given out at the back as was taken in at the front. Who was right?

[57] *Answers: page 91*

CHEAP FLIGHTS

A new airline was starting up with great hopes for the future. The airline owned a fleet of helicopters and offered to take passengers anywhere on the same line of latitude at very low cost.

Their idea was that the helicopter should simply hover in the air and wait for the earth to rotate until the destination is below, and then land.

Why has nobody used this method before?

MARKING TIME

'And this,' said the scientist proudly, 'is our newest caesium clock, the most accurate in the world. If left running for 3000 years it would still be within 1 second of the correct time.'

The visitor, being a taxpayer and mindful of how much money was involved, was determined to be unimpressed.

'My watch,' he said, 'loses two minutes every day, which means that if it is left uncorrected it will be exactly right once every year, whereas your clock is only right once every 130 million years, or so. Anyway, wouldn't a sundial be cheaper and more accurate?'

How did the scientist answer?

ICE OF SPADE

Justin Thyme, the wise old sage of a gardener, had left one of his spades out one frosty night.

'Oh dear!' he thought when he saw it next morning, 'And it was in mint condition too.'

Picking it up by the metal blade, he noticed how much colder the metal felt than the wooden handle.

'Now I wonder why the metal is at a lower temperature than the wood,' he pondered, as he strolled off.

FRED FORTITUDE'S DREAM

Fred Fortitude had a dream that he landed on an apparently uninhabited planet which had the same mass as the Earth. However, he soon discovered that the planet was hollow and the inhabitants lived inside with their heads pointing towards the centre.

In his dream, life on this planet seemed to be little different from life on Earth, except that the ground appeared to curve upwards instead of downwards, and there was therefore no horizon.

Would life on such a planet be as Fred Fortitude dreamed?

 Answers: pages 92/3

COLOUR MIX-UP

Eddy Curran was helping his local amateur theatre group by offering to set up and work the stage lights for them.

For one scene the stage had to be bathed in green light, and Eddy was horrified to find that he had no green filters. Remembering from his art lessons that blue and yellow made green, he put yellow filters in some of the lights and dark blue filters in the rest.

When switched on the lights gave a total effect of white light, much to Eddy's surprise.

What should Eddy have done?

WHEEL MEET AGAIN

Chris Crossbar was enjoying a pint of beer with his friend, Joe Porter, who worked on the railway.

'Wheels are strange things,' philosophised Joe, 'have you ever wondered how they make a vehicle move forward when the part in contact with the ground is always stationary?'

Chris could not say that he had ever thought about it and was quite perplexed by the problem.

'Did you know,' continued Joe, 'that there is a part of a train that is always moving backwards as the train moves forward?'

Chris did not know this, and was now doubly perplexed – can you help?

A PROBLEM OF SOME GRAVITY

Fred Fortitude had been captured by alien creatures. From where he lay, bound and gagged, he could see the surface of a planet from out of the space-ship's porthole.

When the ship blasted off the acceleration pushed him towards the floor as the gravity apparently increased. Fred Fortitude then lost consciousness for an unknown length of time.

When he came round, the apparent force of gravity was still increasing. Just when Fred thought he could stand it no longer, the ship jolted and his weight remained constant at about five times its original value.

Dragging himself to a porthole Fred was surprised to find that the ship had landed once more. Can you explain these observations?

ROLLING STOCK

Professor Spark invented a new propulsion unit for a railway engine.

Large metal balls were rolled down a ramp *inside* the engine. They struck the front of the engine, pushing it along.

Is this feasible?

 Answers: pages 92/5

Solutions

THE TOWING PROBLEM

Mother was quite correct, although it would be a dangerous task to tow the car any distance.
Father had forgotten that the towed car would not be in gear and would be easier to move than if the engine was turning.

WELL...?

Neither is correct. Heavier objects have a greater force of gravity acting on them, but are more difficult to accelerate.

The result of this is that all objects fall with the same acceleration (disregarding air resistance).

WELL IN THAT CASE...?

The air resistance on a falling object increases as the speed of the object increases. Eventually the force of the air resistance equals the weight of the object, acceleration ceases, and the object continues at a constant ('terminal') velocity.

This point would be reached quickly by the light ping-pong ball, and its terminal velocity would be much lower than that of the stone.

The stone would therefore fall faster than the ping-pong ball, but the effect is still due to air resistance.

A BRIGHT IDEA FOR CHRISTMAS

If one bulb failed almost twice the normal current would pass through the opposite bulb. This bulb would soon blow too, causing the whole system to fail.

MARY'S MIRROR

An image is as far behind a mirror as the original object is in front. What a mirror is doing, in effect, is reversing back to front, therefore. (If this were not true, you would see the back of our head when you looked into a mirror!) As a result your image appears to be reversed left to right, but not upside down.

A WAVE OF UNCERTAINTY

An object floating in water does have a circular motion as the wave passes, and is not carried along by the wave. This is because the water molecules in the wave move up and down, not forward.

Surfers catch the wave as it travels into shallow water and 'breaks', during this time the water molecules are moving forward, and are able to push the surfer along.

IMPRACTICAL JOKE

Light rays from all points in the distance enter the binoculars at all points on the lens. So blocking out part of the lens would not block out any part of the image to produce the silhouette effect that Tim had hoped for.

The only effect would be to reduce the brightness of the image, since less light would be entering the binoculars.

SAILING WITHOUT WIND

Unfortunately, Mr Jones had to row all the way back to the shore. The family, and therefore the boat, tended to move backwards as they blew (just as a rocket moves forwards when its jet of gas moves backwards).

This backwards motion cancelled out the forwards motion of the boat caused by the wind hitting the sail.

TIME AND TIDE

The water on the side of the Earth facing the moon bulges towards the moon because it is the nearest and therefore experiences the strongest gravitational force.

Meanwhile, the water on the other side of the Earth bulges away from the moon because it is farthest from it and therefore the gravitational force is weakest.

IRATE PIRATE

A firing angle of 45° gives the maximum range.

For firing at close targets two angles could be employed. A shallow angle causes the cannon ball to have a large horizontal velocity and a small vertical velocity when striking the target. This would be likely to demast the ship or hole it above the water line.

A large angle of firing, however, causes the cannon ball to be travelling downwards as it hits the target and so it would be more likely to go through the bottom of the ship.

The gunnery officer therefore chose the latter angle.

THE INFINITE BALL GAME

In theory, a ball will make an infinite number of bounces before coming to rest. However, each bounce will take less time than the previous one with the result that these infinite bounces are completed in a finite time.

FAITH, HOPE AND CHARABANC

The solution is best visualised by first assuming that there is only one bus plying backwards and forwards.

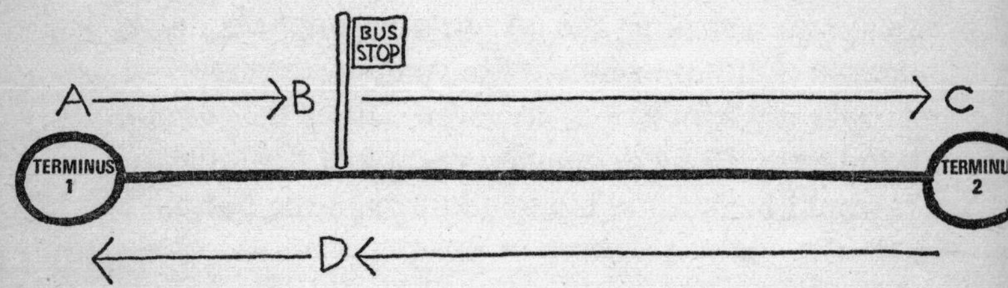

On Grumble's arrival at the bus stop the chances are that the bus is between B, C and D, and so will arrive travelling in the direction CD.

With more than one bus the chances are still that the first bus to arrive will be travelling in the direction CD.

AN ENGINE FAILURE?

All forces come in pairs, which are equal and opposite. When walking, for example, the foot pushes backward, and as a reaction to this the ground pushes forward. (If this did not happen the foot would slip.)

In the same way the rocket which Zxcvbnm invented would move forward in reaction to the expulsion of exhaust gases.

WHY ALTERNATING CURRENT?

Mains electricity is transmitted at very high voltages in order to reduce losses in the transmission lines caused by the heating effect of the current. This voltage has to be reduced by transformers before we can use it at relatively low voltages. Transformers will only work with alternating currents. Furthermore, a generator produces alternating current, which would have to be converted to direct current before it left the power station.

MAROONED IN SPACE

Zxcvbnm would have to use the same principle that worked his rocket, and throw something in the opposite direction to the way he wanted to go.

For example, he could hold his breath, disconnect his breathing apparatus and, either squirt the nitrous oxide away from the ship, or throw the whole apparatus in that direction. As a reaction to this movement he would drift back towards the ship.

TOM'S FISHING PUZZLE

Tom found that the spring balance read neither nought nor two kilogrammes but one kilogramme. The arrangement is basically the same as when he weighed one fish, the fish was pulling down and Tom was pulling up by the same amount. In other words, a spring balance will read one kilogramme if there is a one kilogramme force pulling in both directions.

RECORD WEAR

There are several possible reasons for this. The needle moves faster in the outside grooves, causing more wear. Careless handling is also likely to cause the outer part of the record to be touched. Thirdly, misplacing the needle on the first track of the record could cause minor scratches.

A SHOCKING OCCURRENCE

It is not the voltage that causes harm, but the current flowing through you. If you have a good grip on something live, or if your conductivity is increased by, for example, being wet or in bare feet, the effect of the current is more likely to be fatal.

THE MINE SHAFT

Mrs Jones' weight is caused by every part of the Earth attracting her. Once she started to climb downwards some of the world would be above her and would therefore pull upwards on her; so her weight would decrease. At the centre there is as much of the world 'above' her as there is 'below' and so she would weigh nothing. As she climbed up the other side her weight would increase once more, until her weight was normal on emerging in Australia. In fact we weigh most on the surface of the Earth.

IN HOT WATER

Thick glasses are more likely to be damaged by heat than thin ones because glass is a poor conductor of heat. The part of the glass in contact with the hot water expands while the cooler parts do not. This internal tension can crack the glass.

A CIRCULAR ARGUMENT

Both the track and the train would move, but in opposite directions. The relative velocities would depend on the mass of the train compared with the mass of the track.

POLAR PROBLEM

Time is more complicated than the Geography teacher led Mary to believe. The world is divided for man's convenience into time zones. People in these zones agree to use the same time. If this were not so the clocks in, say, Norwich would be different from those in, say, Cardiff.

At the North Pole there is no day and night as elsewhere, the days and the nights each last six months. Anyone living at the pole would live his life according to a time zone of his choice.

PIGEON PYLON

The difference in voltage between the live wire and the earth is 30,000 volts, and if the pigeon had been able to place one foot on the wire and the other on the earth the current flowing through the bird would have killed it. However, the difference in voltage between the bird's legs when perched on the wire would be so small that there would be a very small current indeed, causing at most a slight tingle.

GLOOM ROOM

An object which is *perfectly* black absorbs *all* the light which lands on it and can, therefore, only be seen in silhouette against something lighter. If everything in a room is perfectly black, then nothing can be seen, no matter how much light there is.

While photographs are being developed certain colour lights are 'safe' and one needs as much of this light as possible. The best colour for a dark room is white.

DECIDING WHAT TO TAKE

The matches would certainly not work without air. Without gravity, the match would quickly go out because there would be no convection current to provide a fresh supply of oxygen.

The watch would work in both situations, but the grandfather clock needs gravity to make its pendulum swing (the length of the pendulum would have to be shortened or the clock would run slow because of the reduced lunar gravity).

A light bulb will not work if the air gets into it, but will work in a vacuum, and a watering can needs gravity. Both of these will therefore work on the moon but not in the space-craft.

The helicopter needs air to fly, and so would not work on the moon's surface.

THE WALL-OF-DEATH RIDER

As Hairy Harry would no longer be moving in a circle there would be no force to keep him on the side of the wall. He had to go hungry.

A FISHY FOUNTAIN

Capillary action is caused by the molecules of the glass attracting the molecules of water, causing the water level to rise. Thus the water will only rise as far as the top of the broken tube.

RED AND ANGER

One set of lights must be at red while the set controlling the other flow of traffic is, in turn, red and amber, green, amber, and red. So it is impossible to design a set of lights where the green is on longer than the red for both streams of traffic.

A PROBLEM IN SOLUTION

In order to hold the compressed spring together, the string must be under tension, and therefore stretched. As the spring dissolves into the acid, the string contracts, and as it does so gives up its energy to the acid in the form of heat.

The spring will eventually break at some point along its length, and the remaining pieces can then expand, producing heat energy in the same way as the string when it contracts.

The result is therefore a slight increase in the temperature of the acid.

HAIRY HARRY'S HOLIDAY

If the luggage is placed inside the car, it has no effect on the maximum speed. However, the maximum acceleration is decreased because of the increased mass.

If the luggage is placed on the roof-rack, the acceleration is again decreased because of the increased mass, and also because of the increased air resistance.

The maximum speed is achieved when the maximum force exerted by the car's engine equals the total resistive forces on the car at that speed. The greater the air resistance, therefore, the lower the speed at which this situation is reached.

RADIANT COLD

The large ice cube prevented some heat from reaching the thermometer, which continued to radiate heat. Before the ice cube had been placed there the thermometer had been receiving as much heat as it was losing. Because the thermometer was now losing more heat than it gained the temperature decreased.

PROFESSOR SPARK'S PERPETUAL MOTION MACHINE

The Professor's machine is doomed to failure. The force needed to push the blocks through the valve, against the water pressure, is greater than that supplied by the falling and floating blocks.

THE WEIGH DOWN

As everything in the lift is accelerating downwards at the same rate, they would appear to 'float' weightless. The bathroom scales would therefore read zero.

This is very similar to the situation in an orbiting space-craft, which is under the influence of gravity, but within which everything is weightless.

HAIRY HARRY'S DOGGY DILEMMA

The dog's nodding head obtained its energy from the up and down motion of the car due to uneven road surfaces. Removing the dog would mean that the car would bounce up and down more – in fact, the dog acts as a small shock absorber.

The up and down motion of the dog in no way affects the forward kinetic energy of the car.

FLOATING ICE

Neither was correct. The level of the water stayed the same. Ice is less dense than water, and floats with about eight-ninths below the surface, and one-ninth above the surface. When the ice-cube changed back to water it occupied exactly the same volume as the amount of ice below the surface, so the level stays the same.

WARNING LIGHTS

There may well be some historical reasons for danger signals being red; an association with the colour of blood, for example.

However, if you have ever approached traffic lights in the fog you may guess why red is an excellent choice. Red lights penetrate much farther than any other colour.

This explains why sunsets tend to be red if there is a lot of dust in the atmosphere – all the other colours are scattered.

HAIRY HARRY'S ATTEMPT AT THE LAND SPEED RECORD

As the motorbike's speed increases, air resistance and frictional forces in general, become greater making it more difficult to accelerate further.

There will come a point when the energy used per second in overcoming these forces will equal the power output of the engine. At this point the motorbike will not be able to move any faster, whatever gear ratio is employed.

EDDY'S CYCLE CIRCUIT

Eddy's circuit would only work if both bulbs were equally bright. The brighter the bulb the more current flows through it. In Eddy's system the greater current flowing through the headlamp would make the rear lamp burn too brightly, and eventually burn out.

HARD-WORKING SHELVES?

Tom's original definition is just one way of calculating the work done. When Mr Brown held the bag still he was using energy and was, therefore, doing work. The energy is used up in the form of chemical energy in the muscles of his arm, keeping them firm and rigid so that the bag does not fall.

However, the shelves are permanently rigid and require no energy to keep them so. The shelves, therefore, do no work.

PROFESSOR SPARK'S PERPETUAL MOTION MACHINE, MARK II

No. The water will not rise up the narrow tube higher than the level of the water in the large container. The pressure of the water, not the weight, is important. The pressure of the water depends on its depth, not the shape of the container.

A REEL PROBLEM

If pulled steadily the reel would either stay where it was, slipping on the ground as it rotated, or it would move towards the person pulling. This would depend on the nature of the surface on which the reel was resting. Jerking the cable would be equally unsuccessful.

If the cable was pulled at a great enough angle to the ground, however, the reel would move away from the person pulling the cable.

You can easily try this for yourself with a cotton reel.

RADIO CONTROLLED SPEED

The energy to run the radio comes from the battery. The energy of the battery comes from the engine via the generator.

While the radio is on it takes current from the battery which is replaced by the generator and as a result the engine runs slightly slower. However, this can be overcome by opening the throttle more, and allowing more petrol into the engine.

The top speed of the car would be slightly affected, since the throttle cannot be opened any more at top speed, but the effect would be minimal.

GENERATING NOTHING

The dynamo, which would not be delivering any current, would become very much easier to turn. The dynamo would therefore speed up until the amount of heat energy generated by friction equalled the amount of energy being given to it.

A PROBLEM OF SPEED

To cover the first kilometre at 15 km per hour took Chris Crossbar 4 minutes. Since this is the total time he must take for the whole journey in order to average 30 km per hour, he would have to return at an infinite speed to qualify!

A PROBLEM OF MORE SPEED

Chris was not always travelling faster than, or at the same speed as Frank. While he was held up by the combine-harvester Chris was cycling slower than Frank.

A MINE OF INFORMATION

The man cannot get away from the mine by climbing up or down the rope, for the mine would move up or down at the same time.

If there is no one in the helicopter free to help, the winchman must attempt to climb both ropes at the same time. This would leave the mine behind, and on re-entering the helicopter he should let go of the rope so the mine would drop back into the sea.

A TYRING PROBLEM

Boyle's law is not incorrect, but Tom was wrong to apply it to this situation. The law only applies to a fixed mass of gas. Tom had forgotten that in blowing up the tyre, the mass of gas is not fixed, because extra air is being added.

JUGGLING THE FIGURES

Charlie is correct in saying that the second arrangement represents the least amount of work but this, of course, is irrelevant to the reading of the scales, which would be the same in both cases.

THE SPACE PATROL PROBLEM

One is, perhaps, tempted to say that the best thruster to use is the one pointing away from the alien ship, so that the reaction to its thrust would push the Space Cruiser nearer.

Unfortunately this would make Fred Fortitude's ship travel faster, throwing it into a higher orbit. In this new, larger orbit Fred's ship would take longer to make one complete orbit, despite the increased speed. Thus, the two ships would draw farther apart.

Fred must fire the thruster in the direction of the alien craft. This will decrease his speed, dropping him into a lower orbit where he will overtake the other craft.

PROFESSOR SPARK'S BOUNCE-ABILITY EXPERIMENTS

When a ball bounces it always loses energy, which is why it never bounces to its original height. For a ball to bounce higher it would have to gain energy on the bounce, which is not possible.

If such a ball was made, however, it would bounce higher and higher, and eventually escape from the Earth. On every encounter in space it would gain more energy, until it could smash every planet or solar system it came into contact with. The ball could never be contained in any kind of box or safe, for it would soon have enough energy to break out.

We hope the Professor soon stops his experiments – just in case!

LIKE A STONE?

The density of hot water is slightly less than that of cold water, so the stone would probably sink faster in the hot water.

In the case given, however, the stone would not reach the bottom of the bucket containing the water at 15° F, since at that temperature the water would be frozen!

A POWERFUL ARGUMENT

The foreman was incorrect in saying that the coil would rotate faster in a stronger magnetic field.

The two extremes are (1) the coil flying to pieces and burning out at about 20,000 revolutions per minute in a very weak field, and (2) the coil slowly smouldering and melting as it tries to move in an unbelievably strong magnetic field.

The energy of rotation comes from the source of electricity.

FRED FORTITUDE'S BEER

The surface of a liquid is not flat, but spherical, and is parallel to the planet's surface. As the moon is smaller than the Earth, its surface is more curved. The surface of the beer in the mug on the moon is therefore also more curved and the mug holds more beer.

However, the extra beer is exceedingly small and not worth the extra expense of a trip to the moon.

HAVING A SWINGING TIME

Initially, the swing time would increase as the bob's centre of gravity became lower. This would eventually reach a maximum.

After this the time would decrease again until all the water had gone. When this had happened the centre of gravity would be in the centre of the bob once more and the timing of the swing would be back to normal.

A MONTHLY ECLIPSE?

The moon orbits the Earth at an angle. Only on rare occasions is the moon directly in line with the sun and the Earth.

This causes an eclipse of the sun when the moon is between the sun and the Earth, and an eclipse of the Moon when the Earth is between the sun and the moon.

WIRING A SKYSCRAPER

Eddy had to make one trip up and one down the stairs.

He started by twisting together two of the wires at the bottom, the third wire he labelled '1'. He then went up the stairs and, with his continuity meter found the two leads that were connected together at the bottom. He labelled these '2' and '3', and the other lead '1'.

Before going down again, he twisted leads '1' and '2' together. At the bottom he untwisted the previously connected wires and found which one of them was connected to the one labelled '1', this must be '2' and the other he labelled '3'.

THE DAIRY'S DAY

The scheme would work in theory. The energy comes from the weight of the milk at the top of the hill. This is mainly water, that comes originally from rain. The rain comes from water evaporated by the sun. So the dairy manager would be powering his fleet of floats by solar energy.

HIGH SPEED HIJACK

The statement is not true.

The bullet travels 1200 km.p.h. faster than the gun. So as the bullet is really travelling at 3600 km.p.h. it would appear to approach the pilot at its normal velocity.

ROAD NARROWS

The cars do behave in the same way as the water: in both cases the rate of flow would be greater if the narrowing were not there at all.

The traffic warden observed that the rate of flow of traffic along the road was slower than usual. However, if there is a steady flow of cars, there must be as many cars coming out of the narrowing as there are going in to it. Therefore, the rate of flow of cars in the narrowing must be the same as the rate of flow before it. Since the road is only one lane wide at the narrowing the cars must go twice as fast through the narrowing as they do approaching it.

A PROBLEM OF WEATHER?

The white snow causes most of the sun's heat to be reflected. The soot would absorb more heat and start the snow melting. Once melted the water would absorb sufficient heat to keep the process going.

The result would be that more of the sun's energy would be absorbed by the Earth, thus making the sea, and therefore the land, warmer.

As the ice-cap at the North Pole is floating it would have little effect on the level of the world's seas and oceans*. However, the ice cap at the South Pole is on land, and melting that would cause extensive flooding.

* See the 'Floating Ice' puzzle.

A TRAIN OF THOUGHT

The guard travelled a greater distance equal to the length of the train. Thus his average speed was greater than that of the passenger sitting for the whole journey.

A SLOWER TRAIN OF THOUGHT

In twelve minutes the train will have travelled two kilometres, and the train itself must also be two kilometres long. Therefore the two stations must each be two kilometres long, as well as adjacent to each other. The man stayed at the intersection of the two stations.

THE SHOOTING LESSON

The reaction would be transferred through the tree to the earth. In fact, the whole earth would move backwards. However, since the velocity of the recoil decreases with mass and the mass of the world is so large, the movement would be too small to measure.

GUN WITH THE WIND

At the instant the bullet strikes, either the vane is distorted by the bullet, or the bullet is distorted by the vane, depending on which is the harder material.

The bullet's forward motion continues while this distortion takes place. During this time the vane accelerates to the final joint velocity of itself and the bullet.

THE SPINNING WORLD

The answer is that gravity prevents this from happening. The Earth would have to rotate once every one and a half hours or so, to prevent gravity holding objects down. If this happened the planet would break up.

People do weigh slightly less at the equator than at the poles because of the rotation of the Earth. About 0·5% of one's weight apparently disappears.

THE RAILWAY CARPENTER

The plumb-line only apparently swings outwards. The weight at the end tries to continue in a straight line as the train turns. The liquid in the spirit level would also try to continue in a straight line and so the bubble would move towards the inside of the circle round which the train was travelling.

The carpenter would not have the same trouble on board an aircraft because a plane banks when it turns.

A FLASH OF INSPIRATION

The idea would work, provided the mirrors were perfect. However, all mirrors absorb some of the light which lands on them, and because light travels so fast (almost 300,000 km.p.sec.) all the light would be absorbed in a very short time because of the number of times the light strikes a mirror.

WAGONS ROLL

Films are made up of many still photographs shown in very quick succession. Between the still photographs of the film in question the wheels rotate just enough so that the spokes appear to be in exactly the same position each time. This gives the effect that the wheels are not moving.

The wheels appear to move slowly backwards when the wagon slows down, because the spokes do not quite reach the same position in the interval between the photographs.

WEIGHTLESSNESS

The scales would read twelve kilogrammes. The water pushes up on the wood to support its weight. The weight of the wood is still pushing downwards on the water, however, and this would register on the scales.

THE HUMMING BIRD

With the wire cage, the spring balance would read about $1\frac{1}{2}$ kilogrammes-force, but with the perspex cage the force of the downdraught on the bottom of the cage would equal the weight of the bird, so the balance would read 2 kilogrammes-force.

If the experiment were performed in a vacuum, the bird would not be able to fly, since it is air flow over its wings that keeps it in the air.

COOLING DOWN

Neither was correct, but the manager was nearer the truth. More heat is in fact given out at the back of the fridge, the extra energy coming from the working of the electric motor, etc. Therefore the chef was increasing the temperature of the kitchen by his actions.

CHEAP FLIGHTS

A hovering helicopter will remain stationary relative to the air. Most of the world's air is dragged round with it. If this were not the case there would be winds of over 1600 km.p.h. at the equator. Therefore, like a hydrogen balloon, the helicopters would be at the mercy of the wind.

MARKING TIME

What is important is the acuracy of timing the interval between two events, and for this the caesium clock is the best. If the visitor's argument was valid the most accurate clock would be one that did not work at all, because it would be exactly right twice a day.

A sun-dial is not very reliable. The Earth does not orbit the sun in a perfect circle, nor at a constant speed. The result is that the sundial is exactly right only four times a year; on other days it can be up to sixteen minutes fast or slow.

ICE OF SPADE

The metal and wood arc probably at the same temperature. However, the metal *feels* colder because, as it is a better conductor; it takes heat away from the hand faster.

FRED FORTITUDE'S DREAM

There would be no resultant gravity inside such a planet, since at any point inside, the gravitational force from one half of the planet is cancelled out by force from the other half. The inhabitants would therefore float around helplessly.

COLOUR MIX-UP

Lights are not like paints. If many different coloured lights are switched on together the total effect is white light. If many coloured paints are added together the total effect is black paint.

Eddy should have put a yellow and a light blue filter in *each* lamp.

WHEEL MEET AGAIN

The fact that the part of the wheel in contact with the ground is stationary is not relevant. What is important is that the wheel should exert a force on the ground. (When one walks the foot remains in one position on the ground while exerting a force backwards.)

The part of the train which is always moving backwards is the lowest part of the outer flange of the wheel. This happens because it is lower than the point where the wheel rests on the rail.

A PROBLEM OF SOME GRAVITY

During the time when Fred Fortitude was unconscious the ship stopped accelerating and everyone on board became weightless. The ship then approached another planet, turned round and fired its retro-rockets to slow the ship down. During this time, when the apparent weight of everyone on board was increasing again, Fred must have recovered his consciousness.

When the ship landed the weight of everybody was normal for that planet. The force of gravity on this second planet must have been five times greater than on the original planet.

As the balls rolled down the slope, the engine would move backwards and stop dead as the balls struck the wall. The train would therefore move backwards in a series of jerks.

You could try this for yourself with some simple apparatus, such as a cardboard box, a tray, a bottle of washing up liquid and some pencils.